WHO WAS NAPOLEON BONAPARTE

Biography Books for Kids 9-12

Children's Biography Books

BABY PROFESSOR
EDUCATION KIDS

Speedy Publishing LLC

40 E. Main St. #1156

Newark, DE 19711

www.speedypublishing.com

Copyright 2017

In this book, we will be learning about Napoleon Bonaparte. He was the Emperor of France, known for being an exceptional military commander who conquered most of Europe. He was born in Ajaccio, Corsica, France on August 15, 1769 and passed away at St. Helena, United Kingdom on May 5, 1821. Read further to learn more about his younger years, his military rule, and his death.

WHERE DID HE GROW UP?

He was born with the name Napoleone di Buonaparte on August 15, 1769. Carlo Buonaparte, an attorney that represented Corsica, was his father and his mother was Maria Letizia Ramolina. He had three sisters and four brothers, which included an older brother, Joseph.

Carlo Buonaparte

Maria Letizia Ramolino

EARLY LIFE

Since his family was fairly wealthy, he could attend school and obtain a decent education. He enrolled at a religious school in January 1779. The following May he started at Brienne-le- Château in their military academy. Corsican was his first language, so he would usually speak French with a Corsican accent and never could spell French correctly. The other students would tease him about his accent so he applied his studies to reading.

Once he completed his studies in 1784 at Brienne, he was admitted to the exclusive École Militaire in Paris. He had been trained as an artillery officer, but upon his father's death and their income being reduced, he had to finish the two-year course in a year. He became the first Corsican graduating from this exclusive school. Pierre-Simone Laplace, a well-known scientist, tested him.

École Militaire

French Revolution

THE FRENCH REVOLUTION

The French Revolution took place in Paris, France while he was in Corsica. The French citizens rebelled against France's King and took over control of their country. Many aristocrats, including the royal family, were killed.

When he returned, he took up with group of revolutionaries that went by the name Jacobis. Napoleon was named the artillery commander during the 1793 Siege of Toulon. The British troops had occupied this city and the British Navy took control of the port.

He developed a strategy to help defeat the British and was able to force them from the port. His leadership during the battle was then recognized by leaders of France and he received a promotion at the age of 24, to brigadier general.

MILITARY COMMANDER

Two days after he married Josephine de Beuharnais on March 9, 1796, he left Paris and took command over the Army of Italy. After a series of quick victories at the Motenotte Campaign, Napoleon able to take Piedmont out in two weeks. They then began to focus on Austria for the rest of the war, which the prolonged struggle for Mantua became the highlight.

Josephine de Beauharnais

Battle of Rivoli

Even though the Austrians started a series of offensives to stop the siege, Napoleon was victorious over the battles of Rivoli, Arcole, Bassano, and Castiglione. The triumph of France at Rivoli taking place in January 1797 was the victory that led to Austria's collapse in Italy. During this siege, France lost about 5,000 men and the Austrians lost around 14,000.

The application of his conventional military ideas to situations in the real world is what made him so victorious, including the innovative use of artillery as a mobile power to assist his infantry.

Battle of Arcole

Battle of Castiglione

He was able to win the battles by concealing troop deployments and concentrating his forces on the "hinge" of the enemy's weak front lines. If this didn't work, he would take a position to the center and then attack the two aligned forces at the hinge, turn around to fight one until left, and would then turn and face the other.

During this Italian campaign, his army was able to capture 150,000 prisoners, 170 standards, and 540 cannons. France's army fought 67 actions, winning 18 pitched battles using their exceptional artillery technology and Bonapart's strategies.

Battle of Friedland

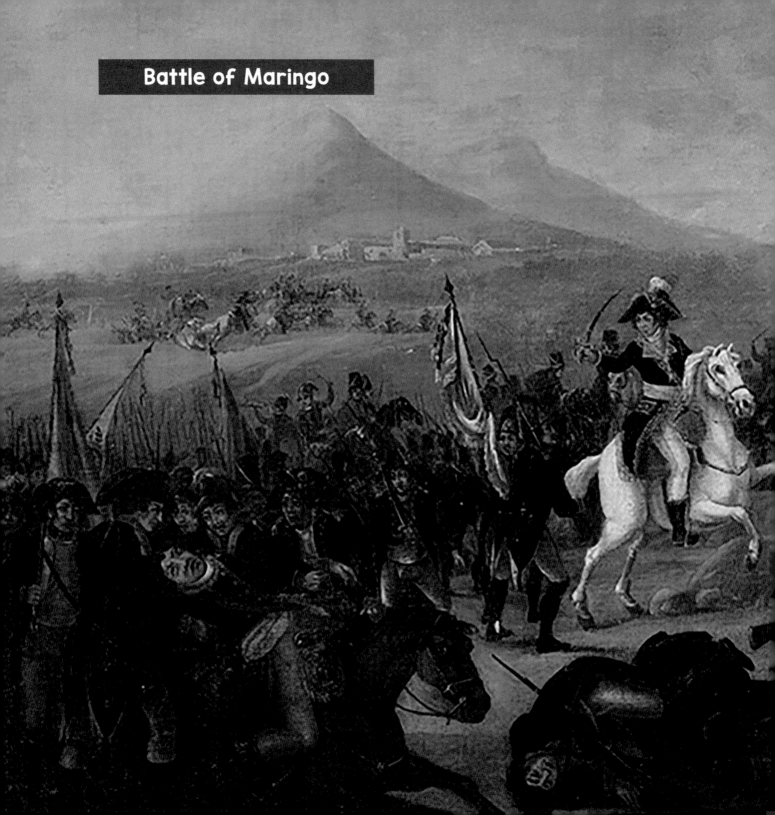

Battle of Maringo

He became more and more influential in French politics during the campaign. He started two newspapers, one for his troops and one for circulation throughout France. He was attacked by the royalists for looting Italy and was then warned that it would be possible that he become a dictator.

When it was all said and done, his forces were able to extract approximately $45 million of Italy's funds during that campaign, $12 million worth of precious jewels and metals, and on top of that, they confiscated over three hundred priceless sculptures and paintings. He then, on September 4, sent General Pierre Augereau to Paris and lead a coup d'état to purge these royalists on 4 September, known as the Coup of 18 Fructidor.

This then left Barras and his allies in control but still dependent on Bonaparte, who went on to negotiate peace with the Austrians. This resulted in the Treaty of Campo Formia, and he then returned to Paris as a hero. He met France's new Foreign Minister Talleyrand, who had served in the identical position for Emperor Napoleon and they proceeded to prepare for the invasion of Britain.

BECOMING DICTATOR AND RULING FRANCE

In 1799, Napoleon returned to Paris after he led a military expedition in Egypt. The political environment in France was in the process of change. The Directory, their current government, had been losing power. With Lucien, his brother, and his allies, he founded a new government named the Consulate.

Napoleon in Egypt

In the beginning, there was going to be three consuls at the top of the government, but he titled himself as First Consul. The powers he had as First Consul then essentially made him the dictator over France.

As dictator over France, he instituted several government reforms. The infamous Napoleonic Code was one of the reforms, stating that government positions would not be based on someone's religion or birth, but whether or not they were qualified and had the ability to perform the position.

This created a major change in France's government. Prior to the Napoleonic Code, top appointments were handed to aristocrats by their king in exchange for favors. This would often lead to people that were incompetent holding important positions.

He was also able to help with improving France's economy with the building of new roads and encouraging business growth. He also was able to reestablish the Catholic Church as the state religion, and at the same time allowing for religious freedom for those that were not Catholic. Napoleon also started some non-religious schools, allowing education for all.

His control and power continued to emerge with his reforms. He was then crowned as the First Emperor of France in 1804. During his coronation, he would not allow the Pope to crown him, but chose to crown himself instead.

CONQUERING EUROPE

In the beginning, Napoleon was able to maintain peace throughout Europe, but France then went to war with Russia, Austria, and Britain. After he lost a naval battle with Britain at the Battle of Trafalgar, he decided to strike Austria. He defeated Austria and Russia soundly in 1805 at the Battle of Austerlitz. During the next years, he was able to expand the French Empire. During 1811, at its greatest extent, France gained control over most of Europe from Spain to the Russian borders, not including Britain.

Battle of Trafalgar

RUSSIAN INVASION

Napoleon made his first real mistake in 1812 when he made the decision to invade Russia. He had a large army march to Russia. Many of the soldiers died of starvation on the way. After an aggressive battle with this Russian army, he proceeded to enter Moscow only to find a deserted city.

The city was soon set on fired, and most of the supplies were gone. As the winter approached, his army then had no supplies and they had to return to France. Once they arrived in France, most of his army died from the bad weather or they died of starvation.

EXILE ON ELBA

Since most of his army was decimated because of the Russian invasion, the rest of Europe then turned against France. Even after a few victories, his army had become too small and was soon forced into exile in 1814 on Elba Island.

THE BATTLE OF WATERLOO

In 1815, he was able to escape from Elba. Napoleon was quickly backed by the army and was able to take control of Paris for a time period referred to as the Hundred Days. However, the rest of Europe would not stand for his return.

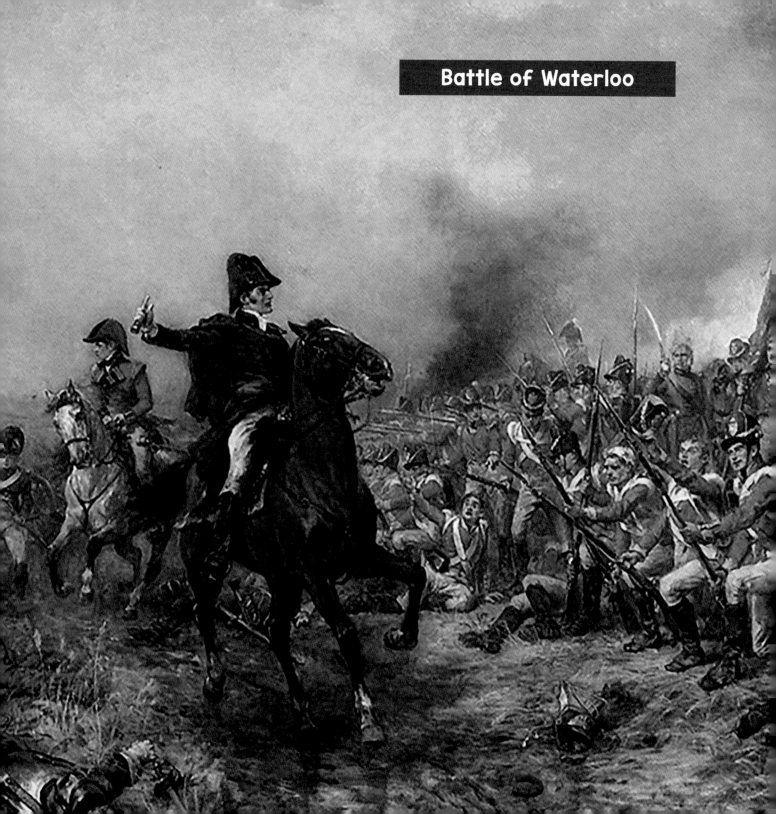

Battle of Waterloo

They proceeded to gather their armies and found him at Waterloo. On June 18, 1815, he was defeated during the Battle of Waterloo and again forced into exile. This time taking place on the island of Saint Helena.

NAPOLEON'S DEATH

On May 5, 1821, Napoleon died after being exiled on Saint Helena for six years. In 1840 his remains were sent to France and on December 15, 1840, they held a state funeral. A procession was held from the Arc de Triomphe through the Champs- Élysées, across Place de la Concorde to Esplanade des Invalides and to St Jérôme's Chapel, where he remained until completion of the tomb.

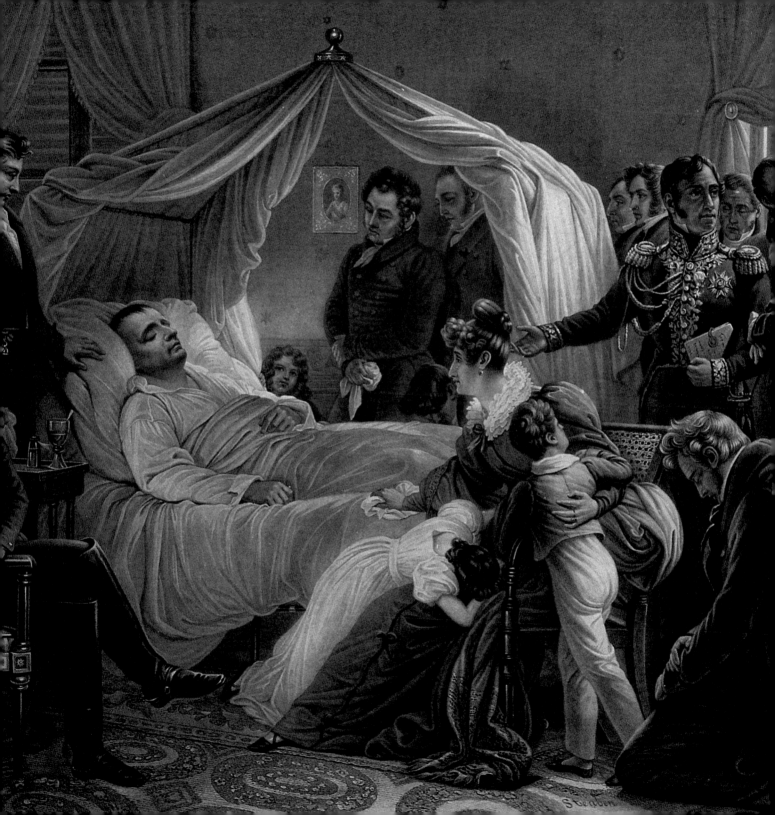

Tomb of Napoleon Bonaparte

His remains were entombed in a crypt under dome at Les Invalides.

Now that you have learned about the life and death of Napoleon Bonaparte, you may want to research the different battles that he was a leader over for additional information.